FIND YOUR TALENT

START A BAND!

Matt Anniss

This paperback edition published in 2014

First published in 2012 by Franklin Watts

Copyright © 2012 Arcturus Publishing Limited

Franklin Watts
338 Euston Road
London NW1 3BH

Franklin Watts Australia
Level 17/207 Kent Street, Sydney NSW 2000

Produced by Arcturus Publishing Limited,
26/27 Bickels Yard, 151–153 Bermondsey Street, London SE1 3HA

The right of Matt Anniss to be identified as the author of this work has been asserted by him in accordance with the Copyright, Designs and Patents Act 1988.

Text: Matt Anniss
Editors: Joe Harris and Sarah Eason
Design: Paul Myerscough
Cover design: Akihiro Nakayama

Picture credits:
Cover images: iStockphoto: Fatihhoca ccl, Jacomstephens tr; Shutterstock: 26kot cl, Bubo cr, Darrin Henry br , Dusan Jankovic ct, Photobank.kiev.ua tl, RoxyFer ccr, Szefei tc, Kachalkina Veronika bc, Buida Nikita Yourievich bl.
Interior images: Alamy: Janine Wiedel Photolibrary 27br; Facebook: 28tcr; Greenwich Photography: 9cr; Myspace: 28tcr; Shutterstock: 26kot 4br; AISPIX 10-11tc; Yuri Arcurs 21tr; Auremar 13t, 19br; Christian Bertrand 5br; Shae Cardenas 16bl; Corepics 23br; Fulvio Evangelista 26-27tc; Eric Fahrner 11cr; Forestpath 9bl; Darrin Henry 26bl; Lia Koltryina 25t; Kzenon 6bl; Aija Lehtonen 4-5 tc, 7tl, 20bl; Randy Miramontez 22bl; Amra Pasic 13t; Losevsky Pavel 18bl; Pixel 4 Images 10bl; RoxyFer 16bl; Dario Sabljak 16r; Adam J.Sablich 3cl, 23tr; Stepanov 29tr; Ronald Sumners 3b, 14cr, 18-19tc; Tamelina 25br; TDC Photography 24cr; Kachalkina Veronika 8cr; Noam Wind 17br; Fabio Venni: 7br.

A CIP catalogue record for this book is available from the British Library.

Dewey Decimal Classification Number 784-dc23

ISBN-13: 978 1 4451 3125 2

Printed in China

Franklin Watts is a division of Hachette Children's Books, an Hachette UK company.
www.hachette.co.uk

SL001935EN
Supplier 03 Date 1113 Print run 3064

CONTENTS

FIND YOUR TALENT!

Standing backstage, you wipe the sweat off your brow and pick up your guitar. Out in the arena, a crowd of thousands is calling for 'one more song'. You turn to your bandmates and give them the signal. This is the moment you have been looking forward to ever since you formed your band!

If you form a band, you could fulfill all of your musical dreams.

Teenage dreams If you have picked up this book, there is a fair chance that the scene above has been played out many times in your dreams. You have probably thought long and hard about getting together with a group of friends to form your own band. It is also likely that you love to be creative and write your own music – songs that you would like to hear on the radio, or see riding high in the CD and MP3 download charts.

Let's go! Across the next few pages, we will explain how you can go about forming your first band, finding musicians and organising gigs. We will reveal the real-life stories behind some of the biggest bands on the planet, and show you how your group can be just like them with a mix of hard work and great ideas. We will even tell you how to find a manager!

The perfect job Maybe you have not dreamed of stardom or writing music, and just want a hobby that could turn into the perfect job. If so, forming a band could be the start of your dream career as a musician.

All the hard work undertaken by artists like Will.i.am is worth it when they hit the top.

EARLY DAYS: The Beatles

Many world-famous bands began their careers as a group of teenagers playing music together in someone's attic or garage. The Beatles' Paul McCartney and John Lennon met at a village fête in Liverpool, where John's band was playing. The two got on well and decided to form a new band. They practised hard in their bedrooms and within a few months, had played their first support slot at a local concert.

FIND YOUR INSPIRATION

What kind of music do you love? This is the most important question to answer before you can form your band and start making music. From rock, indie and synth-pop to heavy metal and hip-hop, you will need to have a clear idea which style of music makes you tick before you begin to look for band members.

Inspirational sound

Some bands stick to playing one style of music, while others become famous for creating a new sound using many different types of music. The stadium dance music act Pendulum owe their huge success to their mix of dance beats, loud rock guitars and catchy pop songs.

Many new bands are as inspired by R&B and hip-hop as rock and pop.

EARLY DAYS: Radiohead

British band Radiohead found fame in the early-1990s with the indie-pop album *The Bends* (1995), but by 2000 they surprised fans with two albums inspired by electronic music, *OK Computer* (1997) and *Kid A* (2000). 'Everyone said you'll sell six or seven million if you bring out *The Bends Part 2*,' guitarist Ed O'Brien told *Rolling Stone* magazine in 1998. 'But we wouldn't do that. The one thing you don't want to say to us is what we should do, because we'll do exactly the opposite.'

GO FOR IT: FIND YOUR BAND

To work out what kind of band would suit you, write down:
- the styles of music you like the most
- your favourite bands
- what you like most about them
- the sorts of clothes and 'look' they have
- which instruments they use

The White Stripes are as famous for their clothes as their music, but they'd be nothing without their great songs.

Great bands such as Green Day combine eclectic influences to make an original new sound.

The music matters

Many new bands spend a lot of time discussing what their band will be called and how they will dress. Don't worry too much about this when you first start out – fans will care more about your music than how you look!

WHO DO YOU THINK YOU ARE?

By now, you should know which musical style your band will have. The next step is to work out your role in the group, and then which other musicians you need to find.

Your band Before you decide which members to include in your group, it might be a good idea to look at the features that make up a great band. For instance, every band needs rhythm, or beats, and bass. Beats are usually provided by a drummer, but sometimes by a computer or drum machine. A bass guitarist most often provides bass.

Drummers are often the butt of musical jokes, but they're the backbone of any great band.

GO FOR IT: PLAY YOUR PART

Decide which of these roles might be best for you:
- front person such as a singer or MC
- band leader but not lead singer
- supporting musician
- a behind-the-scenes musical mastermind who programs music on computers, or writes music, for example

EARLY DAYS: The Beastie Boys

Sometimes, it can take a while for bands to hit the right notes. The Beastie Boys are now one of the most famous hip-hop acts on the planet, but they actually started out as a hardcore punk band. 'We've always listened to a lot of different types of music,' Beastie Boys rapper MCA recently told the Sound Slam website. 'It's nice to be able to play different types of music. Back then, we just wanted a change.'

You can make your music sound original by using an interesting variety of musical instruments.

Alison Goldfrapp makes a great front person for her band because of her charismatic personality.

Your sound Once you have the rhythm sorted, you can think about the music that sits on top of the beats and bass lines. You could go for one or two guitarists and add a keyboard player or even people playing trumpets and saxophones. Your band could be made up of a crew of rappers with backing provided by a DJ. There is no set answer – your band can be anything you want it to be!

BANDMATES WANTED!

Now that you have decided on the make-up of your group, you will need to find bandmates. This might be as easy as getting together with classmates, or it could mean advertising for would-be musicians. Either way, they need to be people who share your passion for music.

Many of the biggest bands on the planet started playing together when they were teenagers.

When looking for band members, be prepared to make new friends and try out people you would never normally consider.

Friends with instruments

The first step when putting together any band is to talk to your friends and classmates. It is likely that some love the same bands or style of music as you. There may be others who play instruments, but have never told you about it. Even if none of your friends are interested, they might know someone who is.

Spread the word Another great way of finding band members is by putting together an advert. Some of the world's most famous bands came together through adverts placed on notice boards in schools, youth clubs or local music venues. Others formed after spotting an advert in a local newspaper, or on an internet music site (there are lots of websites aimed at musicians and would-be musicians).

If your friends have musical talents, try to involve them in your new band.

EARLY DAYS: U2

They now sell out huge concerts around the world, but Irish rock band U2 started life as a schoolboy band. They got together in Dublin after 14-year-old Larry Mullen Junior placed an advert for would-be band members on his school notice board. Six people responded, and soon they were all playing together in Mullen's kitchen in September 1976. Out of this 'jam session', the four-man, and now world famous, band formed.

GO FOR IT: ADVERTISE

Design your own band advert:
- Choose an eye-catching design.
- List the musicians you are looking for e.g. guitarist, bass player, drummer, rapper.
- Describe your style of music.
- Don't forget to add your contact details!

BAND BASICS

With any luck, you should by now have formed your band, and be looking forward to your first band practice. This is when you will have a chance to try out a song together for the first time, and so find out how well everyone in the band can play.

Skill showcase When you get together as a band for the first time, it is a good idea to find out a little more about your bandmates. Before you try playing any songs together, ask each member to show you their skills by playing a song they know well. This is a really great way to work out your bandmates' strengths and weaknesses.

GO FOR IT: PERFECT PRACTICE

The more you practise, the better your band will become. Agree between you:
- when you want to practise
- how long you will practise for
- a timetable that you will all stick to!

It's natural to be nervous when you first perform. Even the most experienced musicians get nerves before a gig.

Oasis went from playing tiny venues to selling out massive stadiums in less than five years.

Get it covered Very few bands can write their own music straight away. A better way to start is to find a song that you all like, and learn to play it. Musicians call this 'covering' a song. You can usually find lyrics and chord lists for popular songs on the internet, while music shops sell sheet music (if you can read music), chord books and many other useful music publications.

INSIDE STORY: OASIS

Being in a band isn't always easy! Many bands split up because they have different ideas about their music. British band Oasis was often troubled by arguments between Liam Gallagher and his brother Noel, who wrote most of the band's songs. The pair fought many times in their 18-year career (often in public), and Noel eventually left the group in 2009 after the brothers came to blows before a big concert.

SORT THE SESSIONS

With the band now up and running, you will need to find yourselves a place where you can practise. There are plenty of places that you could choose from, so take some time to think about what would work best for your band.

When looking for a band practice room, try to find a space you can call your own.

Home comforts In their early days, most bands practise in someone's kitchen, living room or bedroom. While rooms like these can be a good place to start, it is unlikely that family members will be pleased to hear loud music for hours on end! For this reason, garages, basements and attics make better practice rooms.

EARLY DAYS: Public Enemy

Musicians, especially singers and MCs, find all sorts of places to practise. Before they formed the hip-hop group Public Enemy, Flavor Flav and Chuck D delivered furniture for a living. While they carried chairs, tables and wardrobes around, the pair practised their rapping for fun. It paid off – Public Enemy became one of the most famous rap groups of all time.

INSIDE STORY: COLDPLAY

Before they were famous, British rock superstars Coldplay lived together at university and practised in guitarist Jonny Buckland's bedroom. 'Me and Jonny started writing songs in his room,' singer Chris Martin told the Worldpop website in 2000. 'We invited Guy and Will to come and play with us at the flat and slowly we started growing as a band.'

Beyond the bedroom If you can't practise at home, there are plenty of other spaces you may be able to use. Classrooms and school assembly halls might be free after school hours, while church or village halls, scout huts and youth clubs are good options, too. You can even have a look at local musicians' pages on the internet – these often feature lists of cheap or free rehearsal spaces.

Garages offer plenty of space to set up equipment, so they are popular places for bands to practise.

GO YOUR OWN WAY

A s your band practises more, you will be faced with a choice: do you put your own mark on other people's songs or write your own music from scratch? Many of the world's best bands do both, performing a mix of cover versions and their own music.

Many bands write their own songs because they feel they have something to say.

Covering popular songs by artists such as Shakira can be a good way to start out.

Cover up By now, you should have the hang of at least one cover song. If you can play it note-for-note, you are on the way to being a good band. However, unless you can give these songs a twist, you will always be just a cover band.

Write here...write now!
If you can write your own music, the sky's the limit! By composing new songs, using different beats and melodies, you will develop your band's sound and style. You can use a range of samples, such as angry hip-hop lyrics, heavy rock music and fast-beat dance music, and combine them in different ways to suit your band.

GO FOR IT: STYLE IT

Developing your own version of a popular song can be a great way to find your band's voice and style:
- Pick a famous song that the band can play well.
- Throw around some ideas about how you could change it.
- Give it a go – you never know what you might come up with!

Mark Ronson became famous by releasing an album of unlikely, but brilliant, cover versions.

INSIDE STORY: MARK RONSON

DJ and music producer Mark Ronson became famous in 2007 when he recorded Version. It was an album of soul-style covers of indie rock and pop hits by artists such as Britney Spears and Radiohead. 'I would sit down with a guitar or a keyboard and learn the chords from a different song to see what sounded good,' Ronson explained to the skateboard website Crossfire. 'I'd ask myself things like how would I play a Britney Spears song on a guitar? I had so much fun doing those covers.'

WRITE A HIT

The next step in your band's journey is to write your own music. This can seem like a daunting task for beginners, but stick with it – there is nothing more rewarding than writing your very own songs.

Jam hot A good place to start as a band is with a jam session. These sessions can produce melodies, good chord progressions and even entire songs.

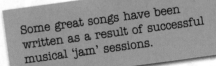

Some great songs have been written as a result of successful musical 'jam' sessions.

EARLY DAYS:
The Kaiser Chiefs

Every song has a story, and the inspiration for new songs can strike at any moment. The Kaiser Chiefs' drummer Nick Hodgson got the idea for the band's hit single *I Predict a Riot* after seeing a big fight outside a nightclub. 'I went home and wrote the riff on the piano and started singing some words,' he said. 'The structure was there, so I took it to the band and then they all wrote their own parts.'

GO FOR IT: JAMMING A SONG

Why not try writing your first song as a band by jamming around lyrics you have written?:

- Write some song lyrics before your band practice.
- At the practice, ask your bandmates to suggest a musical style for the lyrics.
- Work out a rough chord sequence and a melody for the vocals.
- Start jamming around these chords. Try out bass lines, drum patterns and riffs, even keyboard lines and backing vocals.
- Once you have some music, try singing the lyrics over the top.

Your songs will have more meaning if you base them on your own feelings and experiences.

More than words Some songwriters prefer to write the lyrics to a song and then fit music around the words. Some people work in pairs, with one person writing the rhyming words and the other the music. If you're confident enough, you could try to write an entire song, both the music and lyrics – then play it to your bandmates to see what they think.

Two heads are sometimes better than one when it comes to writing music and lyrics.

GOING LIVE

By now, you should be itching to showcase your band's songs by playing them live to an audience. Performing live shows is the high point for many bands.

Nervous energy Even for the most confident new bands, playing your first gig can be both exciting and scary! Some bands deal with the nerves by having a group 'psyching up' session before performing. Others take a few minutes to sit alone and be quiet.

Janelle Monáe is famous for her mesmerising live performances.

Friendly audiences It is a good idea to arrange a small performance in front of friends and family to try out your material. Another option is to put your band forward for a school concert – there will be more pressure, but you will have a bigger audience.

Plan the performance Once you have an audience, you will need to plan a set – a series of songs that show off your band's abilities. When you first start out, you will not need a long set. For instance, at a school concert you may get to play just one song. If you are playing to friends, choose three or four tracks to play.

Invite your friends to hear your first performance – they'll be supportive and give honest feedback.

INSIDE STORY: RAGE AGAINST THE MACHINE

Even experienced bands have bad nights. Some use bad gig experiences to inspire them on to bigger and better things. 'In our early days, we played this show at a hotel in the middle of nowhere and there was no one there...' Rage Against the Machine guitarist Tom Morello told MusicRadar.com. 'We were really low but we had to keep going. When we eventually played at Madison Square Garden in New York, I thought back to that bad gig and how far we'd come.'

GO FOR IT: DUMMY RUN

Try practising your set the night before a performance:
- As a band, run through the set a number of times.
- Each time you practise, go through the set from start to finish without pausing.

GET THE GIG

The next step on your band's journey is to start getting regular gigs. Entertaining crowds of strangers, some of whom could become fans, can be a real high. There's nothing like rocking a crowd with a tight set of your own songs!

Foot in the door Getting your first 'proper' gig can be tough. Wherever you live, it is likely that there will be many other bands fighting for the same few concert slots. You may suffer a few knockbacks before you get your first gig – that is just the nature of the game.

It can be hard securing that first gig, but with a bit of luck you could be playing to a packed crowd like this one.

GO FOR IT: PITCH

The other way to get gigs is to go directly to venue owners and people who promote live music in your area:

- Talk to owners at music venues and music shops. Pitch your band to as many of these people as possible. Take a copy of your demo CD (see pages 26–27), including the name of your band and your contact details.
- Be positive and persuasive when you explain who you are, what style of music your band plays and why you are perfect for a gig!

Rap battle contests can be a great way for new MCs to test out their lyrics.

Talent spotting A great place to start when looking for your 'big break' is a local talent competition. Many venues, local radio stations and concert promoters put on 'Battle of the Bands' competitions for up-and-coming bands, with prizes ranging from guaranteed gigs to money and musical equipment.

EARLY DAYS: The Jackson Five

Before Michael Jackson became a global star, he found fame with his brothers in a group called The Jackson Five. They were first spotted performing in a talent show in their hometown of Gary, in Indiana, USA, when Michael was just eight years old. They were then offered a number of gigs at local clubs and within a year had signed their first record contract.

'Battle of the Bands' style contests offer vital gig slots for new and up-and-coming groups.

ROOM FOR IMPROVEMENT

Getting your first gig is not the end goal for your band, but rather the first step on a path to greater success. If you want to become a great band, you will need to work even harder to improve your performances.

It's not enough to just play your songs – the best bands know how to put on entertaining performances.

Read an audience Most great bands can 'read' their audiences. This means they understand what audiences like about their performances. Here are some top band tips:

- If the crowd likes a certain song, 'extend' (play) it for longer.
- Change your set list depending on audience feedback – go with songs that get a great reaction.
- Listen out for audience feedback when you're playing guitar, drums or keyboard solos. If they love them, use more solos in your shows.

EARLY DAYS: The Black Eyed Peas

When playing live, The Black Eyed Peas noticed that audiences would go crazy for drum solos. Because of this, they now ask drummer Keith Harris to play a different solo every night.
'As far as what I'm going to be playing on the solo, I haven't a clue until I play it,' Harris told Drummer magazine. 'On the last tour, my solos would start the same, but what I actually played in the middle and how I ended it was different every night.'

GO FOR IT
EXTENDING YOUR SONG

All the greatest bands can alter and extend their songs in order to impress audiences. Try doing this in band practice:

- Pick one of your strongest songs and start playing it.
- When you come to a favourite part, give the band a signal to keep going on this course.
- Ask the band to keep playing the same section until you signal them to move on.
- Try this several times with different sections of the song.

To get better as a band, you'll need to learn how to read and respond to audience feedback.

Family feedback It can take a while to learn how to read an audience, so a quicker way to get that information is to ask friends and family who have seen you perform live. Ask them to honestly judge your performance, detailing what they thought was good and what could be improved.

Great singers and rappers get their audiences on side by interacting with them.

DO A DEMO

Once you have written a song or two and have finely tuned your cover versions, the next step is to produce your own band recording – known as a 'demo'.

The key Having a great demo recording is the key to selling your band. You can hand your demo to concert promoters, give it away on the internet to gain new fans or send it to record labels to try to get a contract.

Back-up your demo CDs and look after the master copies – if you lose them, you'll have to record them all over again.

If you want your demo to make an impact, you'll have to be prepared to spend a lot of time perfecting your sound.

GO FOR IT: MAKE A DEMO

To record a song you can use software such as GarageBand (for Apple Macs) or find PC alternatives at www.garagebandforwindows.org. You'll need a USB audio interface, into which you can plug your guitar, bass guitar or microphone:

- Plug your instrument into the audio interface, and the interface into your computer (using the USB port).
- Open up the software and start a new track.
- When you're ready to go, begin recording.
- When you've finished playing, stop the recording. You can create a full demo by repeating this process until you have recorded every element of the song from vocals to drums and guitars.

Computer love There are a number of different ways to record a demo, from hiring out studio space to using home studio equipment such as a 'four-track'. The easiest way to make a demo is to record directly onto your home computer using free audio software.

EARLY DAYS: The Arctic Monkeys

A great example of the power of a good demo is Sheffield indie-rock band The Arctic Monkeys. They built up a huge fan base by giving away their demos free on the Myspace website. Their demos were so popular that they were able to sell out venues around the UK before being signed to a record label. They quickly got a deal and their debut album, *Whatever People Say I Am, That's What I'm Not* went straight to number one in the UK charts in 2006.

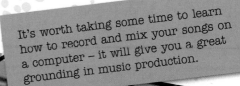

It's worth taking some time to learn how to record and mix your songs on a computer – it will give you a great grounding in music production.

STEP UP A GEAR

Hopefully by now, your band will be gigging regularly and constantly working on new material. Once you have reached this point, the next step is to promote your band in order to start building up a fan base. Here are some ideas for ways you can help your band to take the next step towards superstardom.

Get online Many bands have found success by setting up profile pages on social network sites, where would-be fans can listen to demo recordings. Good examples of band-friendly websites include Myspace, Facebook, SoundCloud and YouTube.

Court the media Your band stands a lot more chance of success if people are writing or talking about you. Send your demos to music reviewers at local newspapers, music bloggers and local radio stations.

Sell your own music The Bandcamp website (www.bandcamp.com) makes it possible for bands to sell their music direct to fans over the internet. It is free to sign up and the site takes just 15 per cent of each sale you make.

Radio DJs play a vital role in promoting new music from up-and-coming bands.

Find a manager Most serious bands have a manager, who helps them by handling gig bookings, pitching their demos to festival organisers, booking studio time and negotiating contracts with record labels.

Some experienced bands manage themselves, but new bands usually ask a family member or an adult friend with business experience to handle their affairs.

If you think you've got talent and could hit the big time, it could be worth approaching an experienced manager. You can find lists of music managers on www.musicsocket.com.

Make some merchandise
Another great way of advertising your band is by selling merchandise such as T-shirts featuring your name or logo. Websites like www.dizzyjam.com will do this for you. It costs nothing to sign up, and for every T-shirt sold you are paid a royalty!

GLOSSARY

advertising the process of telling people about an event or product

audio software a computer program for recording music

band practice a period of time devoted to collectively playing music

bass a musical term for low, booming sounds

bass line a series of bass sounds arranged to complement the rhythm or beats of a song

chord book a publication that explains how to play chords on a guitar or keyboard

chord list a list of guitar or piano chords used in a particular song

chord progressions a term used to refer to planned changes in chord sequences

chord sequences a group of chords played one after another

concert promoters people who organise concerts for a living

debut album a band's first professionally-produced album (collection of songs)

demo CD short for 'demonstration CD' – a homemade disc containing recordings

drum machine a piece of equipment that can be used to create beats

electronic music any style of music made with electronic instruments or equipment

four-track a piece of home studio equipment that allows bands to record four separate instruments at once

heavy metal loud, angry rock music

hip-hop a popular term for rap music

indie short for 'independent', usually used to refer to alternative rock music

inspiration an idea or series of ideas

jam session an unstructured music practice

logo a unique picture used to identify something, such as a band or sports team

lyrics the words of a song

manager a person who looks after the business interests of a band

material a band's songs or music

MC a rapper. Short for master of ceremonies

melodies a sequence of musical notes that form a tune

merchandise products sold by a band such as t-shirts and sweatshirts

music bloggers enthusiasts who write about music on internet blogs

music producer someone who oversees the process of composing and recording music

music reviewers people who assess music for a living

negotiating the process of two or more people discussing a business deal

pitch to enthusiastically explain your skills or products to someone

produce to make something

profile pages website pages featuring information about bands

psyching up preparing yourself or getting in the right mental state for a performance

rapping spoken rather than sung lyrics

record contract a legal agreement between a band and a record label

record label a company that specialises in producing and selling recorded music

riffs short and catchy musical hooks, often played on a guitar

rock a style of music characterised by the use of guitars

royalty money paid when something is sold

sheet music printed notes showing a musician how to play a particular song

showcase a term used to refer to displaying something, such as new songs

signed agreed to something

solo an element of a song played by one musician

stadium dance music popular dance music with a style suitable for performing in big venues

FURTHER INFORMATION

Books

All You Need to Know About the Music Business by Donald S Passman (Viking, 2011)

The Indie Band Survival Guide by Randy Chertkow and Jason Feehan (St Martin's Griffin, 2008)

Six Steps to Songwriting Success by Jason Blume (Billboard, 2008)

Songwriting for Dummies by Dave Austin (John Wiley & Sons, 2010)

Websites

Bandcamp
Sell your music online and create a website for your band:
www.bandcamp.com

BBC New Talent Advice
Read great advice for new bands and musicians from music industry experts:
www.bbc.co.uk/newtalent/music/advice.shtml

Dizzyjam
You can sell band t-shirts, hoodies and other band merchandise for free at:
www.dizzyjam.com

Garageband for Windows
This site is full of information about cheap and free recording software for PC computer users:
www.garagebandforwindows.org

Guitar Chords
A great database featuring lists of guitar chords, progressions and a handy 'chord finding' tool:
www.all-guitar-chords.com

Live and Unsigned
Check out the UK's biggest national competition for unsigned bands:
www.liveandunsigned.uk.com

The Music Business Bible
This site has lots of essential advice about how to get ahead in music:
www.themusicbusinessbible.com

MusicRadar
Take a look at the one-stop-shop for musicians featuring interviews, advice and equipment reviews:
www.musicradar.com

SoundCloud
Upload your demos and find new fans at:
www.soundcloud.com

Apps

Chord Tutor Lite
A free smartphone app for polishing guitar and piano chord skills.

GarageBand for iPad
Try out this easy music creation on the move, for those who want to write songs anywhere!

SoundCloud for iPhone
Record your performance and upload it direct to the music sharing website.

INDEX